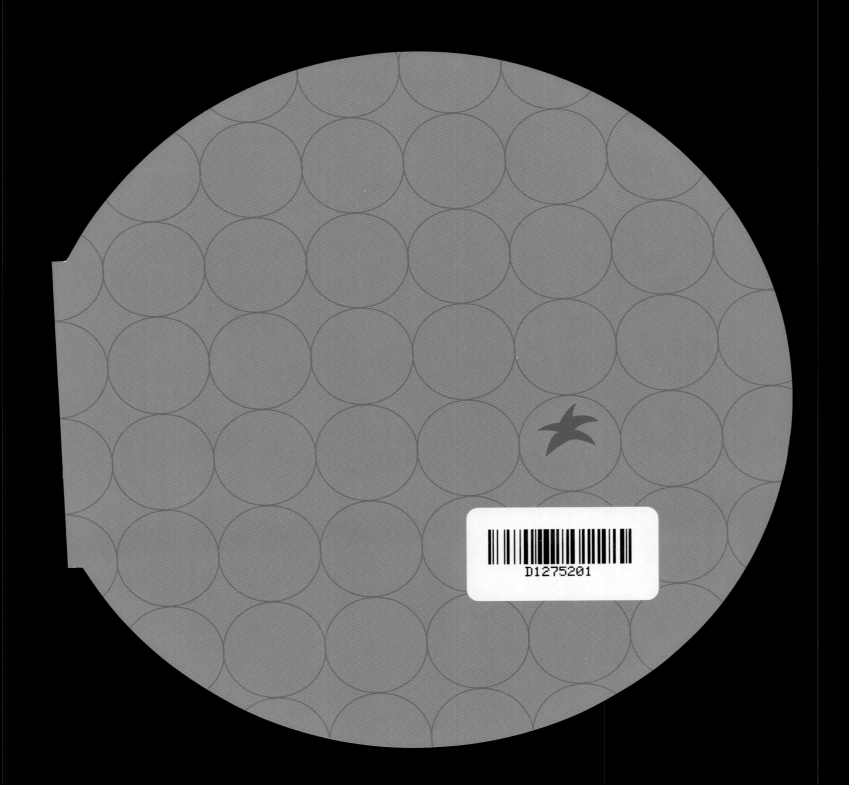

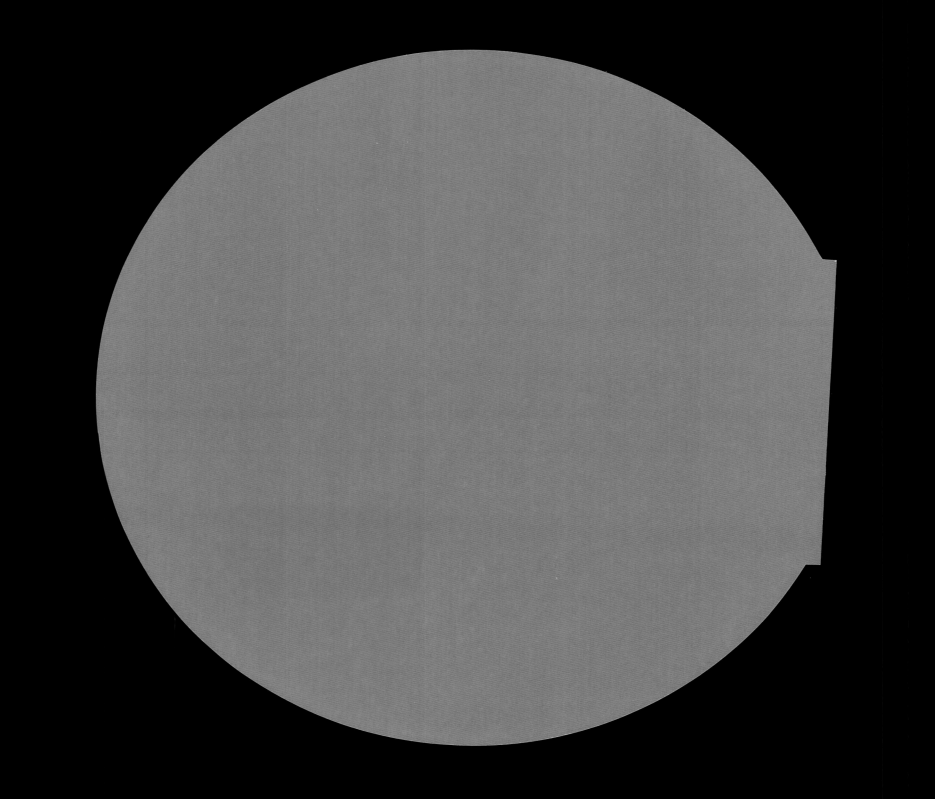

ACADEMIA
BARILLA

TOMATOES

50 Easy Recipes

CREATED BY
ACADEMIA BARILLA

PHOTOGRAPHY BY
**ALBERTO ROSSI
CHEF LUCA ZANGA**

RECIPES BY
CHEF MARIO GRAZIA

TEXT BY
MARIAGRAZIA VILLA

GRAPHIC DESIGN
MARINELLA DEBERNARDI

EDITORIAL COORDINATION ACADEMIA BARILLA
**CHATO MORANDI
ILARIA ROSSI**

CONTENTS

5

THE RED ELEMENT OF MEDITERRANEAN CUISINE

A red sun. Plump, pulpy, and fragrant. It can be eaten raw, on its own or with a little bit of extra virgin olive oil and a dash of salt. It can also be enjoyed in winter as a preserve: a delicious reminder of summer that will enhance any pasta dish and a wide variety of other dishes. The tomato is truly a "pomo d'oro" or "golden apple." Ever since the "tomatl" – its original Aztec name – arrived in Europe from the Americas in the 16th century, it has been used extremely successfully in many dishes in many countries. At first it was thought to be poisonous, and was treated as a simple ornamental plant. Later it was appreciated for the mysterious aphrodisiac virtues it was thought to have, being used in magical potions by alchemists and offered to ladies as a symbol of love. Ultimately it became valued for its unusual sweet yet acidic taste and it spread throughout the whole Mediterranean region. In a climate perfect for its cultivation, the tomato became part of the gastronomic tradition of many cuisines.

Numerous Varieties

It is easy to say just "tomato." In fact there are numerous varieties, all differing in shape and size, each being suitable for a particular culinary use. From the "cherry tomato," small and fragrant, ideal as an appetizer, to the "vine tomatoes," so-called because they grow in a vine like grapes, that are used in many dishes. The "Oxheart" tomato, so-called because of its classic heart shape, is perfect for use in salads, and the "ribbed" tomato that is used in numerous recipes, both raw and cooked. From the "San Marzano" tomatoes, often preserved as peeled tomatoes in cans but also delicious in salads, to the "perino" that is ideal for making passata; from the "datterino", sweet and delicious, and shaped like a date, ideal for eating on its own, to the "Sardinian" tomato, characteristic of the winter, which can be enjoyed raw tomatoes are as versatile as they are delicious. Finally, the most delicious Italian phenomenon: the

several varieties of "Pachino" tomatoes, cultivated in south-eastern Sicily, that have been granted Protected Geographical Status by the Italian Government.

A Force for Our Well-Being

Very tasty, but much more than that, the tomato contains antioxidants; vitamins C and E, betacarotene, and flavonoids. When ripe, it also contains large quantities of lycopene. This is a particularly precious antioxidant: the human body cannot synthesize it, so it can only be absorbed through the few foods that contain it. Tomatoes also have few calories (17 to 20 per 100 g) and it does not lose its organoleptic and nutritional properties, including its high lycopene content, when processed by the food industry into canned tomatoes, purée, and preserves.

King of the Mediterranean

With wheat and extra virgin olive oil, the tomato is one of the basic ingredients of the "Mediterranean diet," recently recognized as an "Intangible Cultural Heritage" by UNESCO. There are no culinary tradition in countries such as Spain, France, Italy, and Greece that do not include tomatoes. Raw, pureed, or dried, fried, baked, stuffed, grilled, gratiné, and candied, in sorbets and chutneys. And to decorate a dish by adding an unmistakable touch of color, tomatoes are included in so many sophisticated recipes, both traditional and new, all over the Mediterranean. Academia Barilla, the international center devoted to the promotion of Italian gastronomy throughout the world, has therefore selected the following fifty recipes. In some of them, the tomato is the undisputed protagonist as in the traditional "Pasta with Tomato Sauce," a simple but delicious dish. In others the tomato is more in the background but its taste and color are so important that if it were missing the dish would lose its identity. Indeed, what would the Caprese salad be without those sunny red slices?

FROM AMERICA AND BACK:
A BRIEF HISTORY OF THE TOMATO

Indeed the tomato is a great traveler. Native to western South America, today the wild tomato or *Solanum racemigerum* still grows in the wild in the mountains in Peru, Ecuador, and northern Chile. It is considered to be the ancestor of all the tomato varieties known today. From the Andean region, it traveled to Central America where it was cultivated by the Mayas who developed the larger fruit we are now familiar with. In turn it was adopted by the Aztecs who cultivated in the southern parts of Mexico. It was here that Hernán Cortés discovered it when he invaded the region between 1519 and 1521. From Mexico the tomato made its way to Spain, probably in the form of seeds, introduced by the settlers and missionaries.

New Foods from the New World

The encounter between the Old World and the New resulted in one of the most extraordinary culinary exchanges in the history of human eating. In 1492 numerous vegetable and animal species, still unknown in Europe, arrived in the Old World in the wake of Christopher Columbus's travels. In addition to the tomato, the new vegetables and other plants introduced into Europe included the chili pepper and several other varieties of peppers, manioc, peanut, potato and sweet potato, varieties of zucchini, sunflower, pineapple, and other tropical fruits, cocoa, vanilla, and tobacco; and among animals, the turkey.

The settlers, on the other hand, arrived in the New World with rice, wheat, barley, rye, oats, lentils, chickpeas, broad beans, chard, artichokes, spinach, carrots, melons, pomegranates, citrus fruits, peaches, cherries, vines, olives, coffee, and sugar cane. All these spread to the south, as well as northwards to North America. The European settlers who wanted to maintain the way of life to which they were accustomed also brought with them numerous animals: donkeys, mules, cows, pigs, goats, sheep, and poultry previously unknown in the Americas.

The tomato appeared in Europe in the first half of the 16th century but people were suspicious of it at first. It was believed that the first varieties contained enough solanine to make them indigestible or even poisonous. As a result they were originally used mainly as ornamental plants, but because they were also thought to have medicinal properties they were also studied in botanical gardens, and their appeal remained limited. It was only as a result of subsequent varietal selection that the tomato became accepted as an edible food.

In Italy

Italy was the first European country after Spain to become acquainted with the tomato. This occurred because of the close relationship that existed on Italian territory. The tomato's "official" history in Italy started in Pisa on October 31, 1548, when families of the time and the Spanish dominions that existed on Italian territory. The Grand Duke of Tuscany, Cosimo de' Medici, received a crate a tomatoes from the Florentine estate of Torre de' Gallo; the seeds had probably been a gift from the viceroy of Naples to his daughter, Eleonora of Toledo, Cosimo's wife. From Sardinia, still ruled by Spain, the tomato reached Genoa, at the time the main port of the Tyrrhenian Sea. From there it spread throughout Liguria thanks to the favorable climate. The tomato then crossed the Apennines and reached the plains of Piacenza, Parma, Milan, Novara, and Turin. The spread of the tomato in Italy was at first restricted to the courts of the aristocracy and to botanical gardens. Since it was believed to be poisonous, it was initially used only as an ornamental plant and its gastronomic potential was completely ignored. It was only in the 18th century that people began "experimenting" with what had for so long been purely an ornamental plant, leading in the 19th century to the widespread propagation of the tomato as we know it today. However the process was a slow one.

9

In Cooking

The arrival of the tomato was not an immediate culinary discovery. New foods that vaguely resembled what people were already eating had a greater chance of being quickly accepted in European cuisine: this was the case with maize, American kidney beans, and chili peppers. In contrast the acceptance of the tomato was slow and difficult.

It was only at the end of the 17th century that the tomato made the move from the botanical garden to the private garden and from there to the kitchen. The first person in Italy to publish a recipe using tomatoes was Antonio Latini. In his book *Scalco alla moderna* ("The Modern Steward") published in Naples in 1694, he recommended that the tomato should be stewed with eggplants and zucchini.

Until then most dishes were dominated by the paler colors of butter, cheese, and béchamel. The "red revolution" started in Sicily and Naples and gradually but steadily spread towards northern Italy. In the second half of the 18th century there were several recipe books with suggestions about using tomatoes but the fruit still remained the prerogative of the wealthy aristocracy. It was only in the 19th century that the historic combination with pasta took place, the traditionally white pasta becoming "red" when dressed with tomato sauce.

Fortunately the encounter between "Maccheroni" and "Pommarola" (macaroni and summer tomato sauce) was not the only one: at the same time the tomato also conquered the pizza. In 1835 Alexandre Dumas (1802-1870) described the various types pizzas, almost all of them still "white." He mentioned ones with oil and garlic, or with anchovies, and, as a small exception, the pizza with tomatoes that was destined to depose all the others in a very short time. In the 19th century the tomato gradually became the "ordinary food" of peasants throughout southern Italy while preserved or puréed tomatoes were slowly becoming established. Continuing its way to the north of Italy, tomatoes and tomato sauce soon replaced bacon fat in the preparation of basic dishes such as soup, rice, and polenta. In 1931 the Gastronomic Touring Guide of Italy declared that the tomato "has acquired citizen's rights in almost all the regions of Italy." The tomato continued its conquest and soon became part of what in 1950 came to be described as the "Mediterranean diet," destined to spread throughout the world once again. And thus the tomato crossed the ocean once again.

There... and Back

In Salem, Massachusetts, there is a monument dedicated to Michele Felice Corne (1752-1845), an Italian painter, born on the island of Elba, who arrived from Naples in July 1800. He became famous, not only for his painting, but for being the first person to have the courage to taste a tomato in America, ignoring the superstition that it was poisonous. So, thanks to an Italian who had appreciated its culinary versatility in Naples, the tomato returned, gastronomically speaking, to the American continent, giving rise to a flourishing food processing industry that is thriving today. In the 1920s the newly appointed director of the "Experimental Station for the Food Preserving Industry" in Parma, the Italian city celebrated for the high quality of its food products and its food industry, which even has a museum devoted to the tomato, visited America. There he went to numerous American food factories to study the advanced technologies used in the production of preserves. The tomato, the child born on the American continent, had returned home. But in the course of its travels the tomato had "married" the Italian and European culinary traditions: indeed, what would a pizza, pasta, and the Mediterranean diet be without tomatoes? Without the Italian gastronomic imagination the tomato might never have found fame and fortune...

Giancarlo Gonizzi
Curator of the **Academia Barilla Gastronomic Library**

11

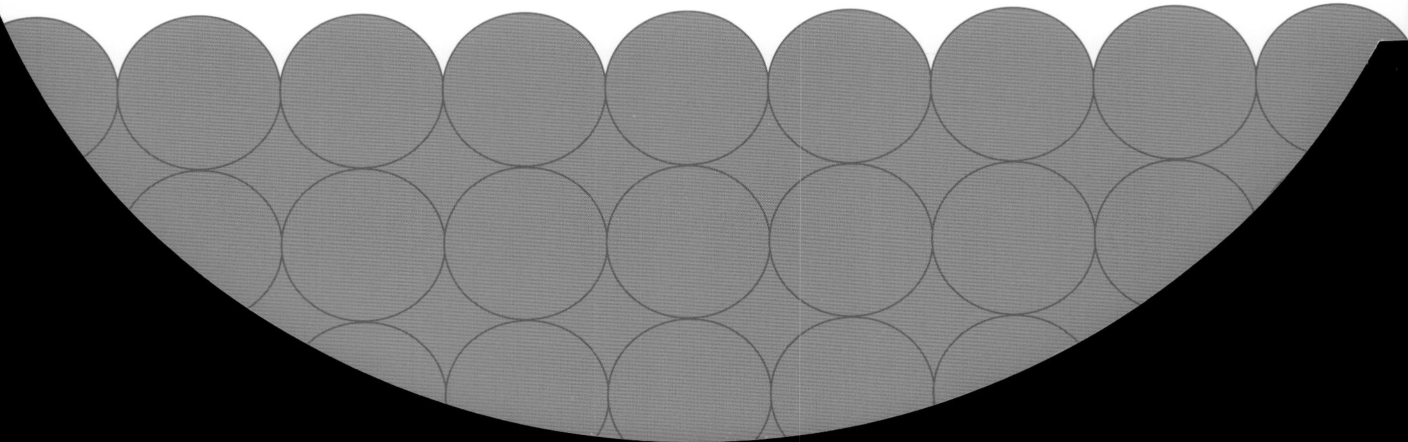

Appetizers

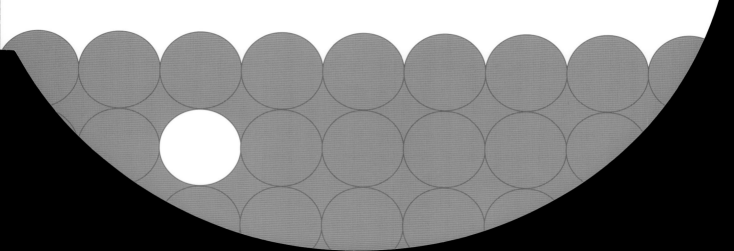

BRUSCHETTA WITH EXTRA VIRGIN OLIVE OIL, TOMATOES, AND BASIL

INGREDIENTS FOR 4 PEOPLE

10 oz (300 g) baguette (1 medium)
1 clove garlic
3 San Marzano tomatoes
1 1/2 tbsp (20 ml) extra virgin olive oil
basil
salt

METHOD

Wash the basil leaves and gently pat dry. Chop coarsely.
Cut the baguette into slices about 3/8-in (1-cm) thick and toast
in the oven or in a frying pan.
Peel the garlic clove. Toast the slices of bread, then rub them lightly
with the whole garlic clove.
Wash, dry and cut the tomatoes into dice. Season with salt,
extra virgin olive oil, and the chopped basil.
Leave the mixture to infuse for a few minutes.
Arrange the tomato mixture on the toasted slices of baguette.
If the slices are large, cut them into smaller pieces.

Preparation time: 20'

SAVORY CAKE
WITH DRIED TOMATOES,
CAPERS, AND OREGANO

INGREDIENTS FOR **4** PEOPLE

3 eggs
2 tbsp (30 ml) extra virgin olive oil
2/5 cup (100 ml) milk
1 2/3 cups (200 g) all-purpose flour
0,5 oz (16 g) brewer's yeast
1 cup (100 g) grated Pecorino
3 1/2 oz (100 g) dried tomatoes
3 tbsp (25 g) capers
1 tbsp (5 g) oregano
salt and pepper

METHOD

Beat the eggs with the oil and the milk, then season with salt and pepper.
Add the flour and the yeast, then mix together. Stir in the grated Pecorino, the
coarsely chopped capers, the dried tomatoes, and finally the oregano.
Butter a mold, sprinkle the inside with flour and
fill it three-quarters full with the mixture.
Bake in the oven, preheated to 360°F (180°C) for 35 to 40 minutes.

Preparation time: 15'
Cooking time: 35-40'

CAPRESE SALAD

INGREDIENTS FOR 4 PEOPLE

1 lb 2 oz (500 g) mozzarella
1 lb 3 oz (600 g) Oxheart tomatoes (4 large)
2 tbsp (30 ml) extra virgin olive oil
basil
salt

METHOD

Wash and dry the tomatoes.
Cut the mozzarella and tomatoes into similar-sized slices and sprinkle lightly with salt.
Wash and gently pat dry the basil leaves.
Alternate the slices of tomatoes and mozzarella, interleaving them with a few basil leaves.
Sprinkle with a little extra virgin olive oil and serve.

Preparation time: 15'

GAZPACHO

INGREDIENTS FOR 4 PEOPLE

2 lb 2 oz (1 kg) vine tomatoes (6 large)
5,3 oz (150 g) red onions (2 small)
4 oz (120 g) cucumber (1/3 large)
4 oz (120 g) celery (3 stalks)
10 oz (300 g) bell peppers (2 large)

1 clove garlic
1 sprig basil
2 tbsp (30 ml) extra virgin olive oil
3 cups (150 g) bread, cubed
salt and pepper

METHOD

Toast the cubed bread in the oven.
Peel the tomatoes and remove the seeds, then cut each into four quarters.
Clean and peel the onion and cucumber. Wash the celery.
Put aside a small piece of each of the vegetables to garnish the gazpacho.
Chop the garlic finely. Coarsely chop the rest of the vegetables, then brown in a pan
with the oil and chopped garlic.
Remove from the heat and add the tomatoes, basil, and bread.
Blend this tomato mixture until smooth, season with salt and pepper,
and place in the refrigerator for at least one hour.
Cut the reserved vegetables into small dice.
Serve the gazpacho very cold, garnished with the diced vegetables.

Preparation time: 20'

BASIL AND TOMATO JELLY
WITH BURRATA CHEESE

INGREDIENTS FOR 4 PEOPLE

1 lb 1 oz (500 g) ripe vine tomatoes (4 medium)
5 oz (150 g) burrata cheese
3 sheets leaf gelatin
extra virgin olive oil
basil
salt and pepper

METHOD

Wash the basil leaves and dry them gently. Chop them finely.
Peel the tomatoes and remove the seeds. Pass them through a food mill
to make a purée (or purée them in a blender).
Season to taste with salt and pepper.
Heat half the puréed tomatoes in a pan until they are warm.
Meanwhile soften the gelatin in cold water, squeezing out as much water as possible, then add to
the tomatoes in the pan. Incorporate this mixture into the remaining puréed tomatoes and
stir in the chopped basil. Carefully pour into small glasses.
Place the glasses in the refrigerator for at least two hours.
When the tomato jelly has set, add a little burrata cheese to each glass.
Season with a dash of extra virgin olive oil, garnish to taste and serve.

Preparation time: 30'
Resting time: 2 h

GRISSINI
WITH TOMATO AND THYME

INGREDIENTS FOR **4** PEOPLE

4 cups (500 g) all-purpose flour
1 1/2 tbsp (25 g) brewer's yeast
1 1/2 tsp (10 g) salt
1 1/2 tbsp (25 g) extra virgin olive oil
1 cup (250) ml water
1/3 cup (80 g) tomato paste
1 tsp thyme leaves

METHOD

Dissolve the yeast in a little warm water. Wash and dry the thyme leaves.
Put the flour on a pastry board and make a well in the middle. Work the tomato paste
into the flour. Stir the dissolved yeast into the water, then pour the liquid onto the flour
and tomato paste mixture and start kneading. When the kneading is almost
complete, add the salt and thyme leaves.
Continue kneading until the dough is soft, smooth, and elastic.
Cover with plastic film and leave to rest for about 30 minutes; then shape
into a long baguette and cut into chunks with a metal spatula.
Preheat the oven to 480°F (250° C). Arrange the grissini on a baking sheet
with space between them and bake in the oven for about 15 minutes.

Preparation time: 30'
Rising time: 30' - Cooking time: 15'

MILLE FEUILLE OF BUFFALO MOZZARELLA AND SEMI-CANDIED TOMATOES

INGREDIENTS FOR **4** PEOPLE

9 oz (250 g) buffalo mozzarella
4 tbsp (60 ml) extra virgin olive oil
4 vine tomatoes
1/2 oz (15 g) basil (about 30 leaves)
sugar
garlic
thyme
salt and pepper

METHOD

Preheat the oven to 210°F (100°C). Wash and dry the tomatoes, then slice them, salt them, and sprinkle a little sugar on top. Bake for about an hour with the finely sliced garlic, thyme, and extra virgin olive oil.
Wash the basil and dip in boiling water. Cool in water with ice cubes, then remove the leaves and blend with 3 1/2 tbsp (50 ml) extra virgin olive oil.
Slice the buffalo mozzarella and season lightly with salt and pepper.
Make the mille feuille by alternating the mozzarella with the slices of semi-candied tomatoes.
Sprinkle a dash of extra virgin olive oil on top and garnish with the basil sauce.

Preparation time: 1 h 10'

NASTRINE WITH DRIED TOMATOES AND OREGANO

INGREDIENTS FOR 4 PEOPLE

FOR THE PASTA
4 cups (500 g) all-purpose flour
1 egg
2 tbsp (20 g) sugar
4 tsp (20 g) brewer's yeast
1 cup (250 ml) water
2 tsp (12 g) salt
5 tsp (25 g) butter

FOR THE FILLING
2 oz (60 g) dried tomatoes
3/4 cup (150 g) salted capers
1 egg
oregano

METHOD

Dissolve the yeast in the water. Put the flour on a pastry board and make a well in the middle, then add the sugar, the egg, and the water, little by little. Incorporate the butter, softened at room temperature, and lastly the salt. Continue kneading until the dough is smooth and elastic. Cover with plastic film and leave in a warm, humid place to rise for about 30 minutes.
Next take a rolling pin and roll out the dough on the floured pastry board to a thickness of 1/8 in (3 mm). Brush with some of the beaten egg. Cut the dried tomatoes into pieces and place them on top. Rinse the capers under running water to remove the salt, then add them as well as a little oregano to taste. Roll the sheet of pastry into a cylinder with the filling inside. Cut into strips 1 to 1 1/4 in (2.5 to 3 cm) long, twist them, and arrange them on a buttered baking sheet. Leave to rise until they have doubled in size (this should take about one hour). Preheat the oven to 400-430°F (200-220°C). Now brush the nastrine with the remaining beaten egg to add a shine and bake in the oven for about 20 minutes.

Preparation time: 1 h
Rising time: 1 h 30' - Cooking time: 20'

TOMATO ROLLS

INGREDIENTS FOR 4 PEOPLE

4 cups (500 g) all-purpose flour
3/4 cup + 1 1/2 tbsp (200 ml) water
1 tbsp (15 g) brewer's yeast
4 1/2 oz (130 g) grape tomatoes
1 1/2 tsp (10 g) salt

METHOD

Dissolve the yeast in lukewarm water, about 35°C (95°F).
Wash the tomatoes and purée them in a blender.
Put the flour on a pastry board and make a well in the middle.
Pour the tomato purée into it and work it into the flour.
Add the yeast and water mixture to the flour and tomato and work it in.
Add the salt when the ingredients are nearly all incorporated.
Continue kneading to obtain a soft, smooth, elastic dough. Cover the dough with plastic film
and leave to rest for 30 minutes. Then make small balls of about 2 oz (50 g) each.
Mould into the shape you like and arrange on a baking sheet, greased with oil,
with enough space between them. Cover with plastic film and leave to rise for about 40 minutes
until they have doubled in volume.
Preheat the oven to 350-375°F (180-190°C). Bake for about 15 minutes.

Preparation time: 1 h
Rising time: 1 h 10' - Cooking time: 15'

MEDLEY OF LITTLE PIZZAS

INGREDIENTS FOR 4 PEOPLE

10 oz (300 g) puff pastry
9 oz (250 g) assorted tomatoes
1 3/4 oz (50 g) Scamorza or Emmental cheese
1/2 oz (15 g) anchovy fillets
1 oz (25 g) pitted olives (about 6 large)
1 tbsp (10 g) capers
oregano
salt

METHOD

Roll out the puff pastry to a thickness of 1/8 in (3 mm).
Cut out discs and prick them with a fork.
Arrange the little pizzas on baking sheet lined with parchment paper.
Wash the tomatoes and cut into dice or purée them.
Cut the cheese into dice.
Garnish the pizzas with the tomatoes, then arrange of few cubes of cheese on top
and decorate with the rest of the ingredients. Sprinkle with a little oregano and a pinch of salt.
Preheat the oven to 410°F (210°C). Bake for about 13 minutes.

Preparation time: 30'
Cooking time: 13'

FRIED
GREEN TOMATOES

INGREDIENTS FOR **4** PEOPLE

1 lb 2 oz (500 g) green tomatoes (3 large)
generous 1/3 cup (50) g all-purpose flour
2 eggs
1 1/4 cups (150 g) breadcrumbs
3/4 cup (200 ml) extra virgin olive oil
salt

METHOD

Wash the tomatoes and cut into slices about 1/4 in (6 mm) thick. Beat the eggs.
Coat them first in flour, then in the beaten eggs, and finally in the breadcrumbs.
Heat the oil in a pan. Add the bread-crumbed tomatoes and fry for about 5 minutes,
turning them with a spatula halfway through the cooking time.
Drain and dry on a paper towel. Add salt and serve.

Preparation time: 15'
Cooking time: 5'

TIMBALE OF BLACK VENERE RICE WITH SEMI-CANDIED CHERRY TOMATOES AND PEAS

INGREDIENTS FOR 4 PEOPLE

2/3 cup (120 g) black Venere rice
3 1/2 tbsp (50 ml) extra virgin olive oil
3 1/2 tsp (15 g) sugar
7 oz (200 g) Pachino cherry tomatoes
1 clove garlic

3 to 4 leaves basil
pinch dried oregano
1/3 cup (50 g) peas
salt and pepper

METHOD

Preheat the oven to 190-210°F (90-100°C). Wash and dry the tomatoes, cut them in half, and season with salt. Sprinkle the sliced garlic, oregano, 1 tbsp (15 ml) extra virgin olive oil on the tomato halves and bake for about 1 hour.
In the meantime cook the Venere rice in salted boiling water for about 30 minutes until al dente, then drain.
Cook the peas in salted boiling water for 2 minutes. Drain and immediately put in iced water to cool.
In a bowl, mix together the rice, peas, and cherry tomatoes. Wash and dry the basil, tear into pieces, then sprinkle on top of the tomatoes together with half the remaining olive oil.
Season with salt and pepper.
Oil four individual molds. Spoon the rice mixture into them and place them in a water bath in the oven until the rice is hot again. Then turn upside down on individual plates and sprinkle with a dash of extra virgin olive oil.

Preparation time: 1 h 10'
Cooking time: 30'

SAVORY TOMATO AND
GOAT CHEESE TORTA

INGREDIENTS FOR 4 PEOPLE

7 oz (200 g) puff pastry
7 oz (200 g) Oxheart tomatoes
2 oz (60 g) Caprino goat's cheese
2/3 cup (150 ml) milk
1 egg

1 tsp cornstarch
2 1/2 tbsp (15 g) grated Parmesan
chives
salt and pepper

METHOD

Roll out the puff pastry to a thickness of about 1/8 in (3 mm). With it, line a cake tin or 4 individual molds.
Wash and dry the tomatoes, then cut them into slices. Cut the goat cheese into slices.
Arrange the sliced tomatoes and goat cheese on the bottom of the tin or the molds.
Meanwhile, wash, dry, and chop the chives. Stir a little milk into the cornstarch. Whisk into it
the egg, the rest of the milk, the grated Parmesan, salt, pepper, and the chopped chives.
Pour this mixture onto the tomatoes and goat's cheese in the cake tin or molds.
Preheat the oven to 350°F (180°C). Bake for 30 minutes,
or a little less if you are using 4 individual moulds).

Preparation time: 20'
Cooking time: 30'

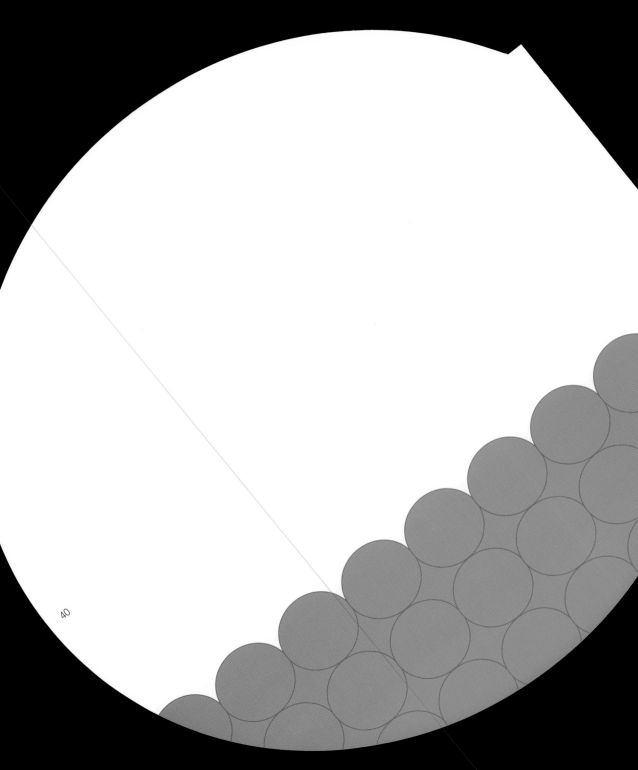

40

First Courses

NOODLES WITH SWORDFISH, CHERRY TOMATOES AND WILD FENNEL

INGREDIENTS FOR 4 PEOPLE

10 oz (300 g) bavette or other thin ribbon pasta
10 oz (300 g) swordfish
10 oz (300 g) cherry tomatoes
3 tbsp (40 ml) extra virgin olive oil
1 clove garlic
wild fennel
chili pepper
salt and pepper

METHOD

Wash and dry the tomatoes, then cut in half.
Cut the swordfish into cubes. Pour a little extra virgin olive oil in a non-stick frying pan, bring it to a high temperature, then add the cubed swordfish and sear. Season with salt, pepper, and the sprig of wild fennel, previously washed and dried.
Pour the rest of the oil into another pan and add the peeled garlic clove, whole, and the chili pepper. Brown lightly. Now add half the tomatoes, seasoned with salt, and cook for another couple of minutes. Add the fish.
Meanwhile, cook the pasta in salted boiling water until al dente, drain and add directly to the pan with the sauce.
Cook lightly for a few seconds, then serve.

Preparation time: 20'
Cooking time: 10'

BUCATINI
ALLA AMATRICIANA

INGREDIENTS FOR **4** PEOPLE

12 oz (350 g) bucatini
6 oz (150 g) pig's cheek or pancetta
4 ripe vine tomatoes
1 red chili pepper
scant 1/2 cup (40 g) grated Pecorino Romano
salt and pepper

METHOD

Cut the pork cheeks or pancetta into slices and then into rectangles. Put in a pan,
add a very small amount of water and simmer so that the fat melts.
Peel the tomatoes, remove the seeds, and cut into chunks. Remove the pork cheek or pancetta pieces
from the pan and drain them thoroughly. Add the tomatoes to the pan in the fat left by the pork.
Season with the crumbled chili pepper and a little salt and pepper. Now return the pork cheek
or pancetta pieces to the tomato sauce in the pan and heat briefly.
Cook the bucatini in plenty of salted water until al dente.
Add the sauce and grated Pecorino. Mix well and serve hot.

Preparation time: 15'
Cooking time: 8'

CONCHIGLIONI WITH SICILIAN-STYLE PESTO

INGREDIENTS FOR **4** PEOPLE

2 1/4 lb (1 kg) Piccadilly or other small plum tomatoes
12 oz (350g) conchiglioni (pasta shells)
generous 1/4 cup (50 g) pine nuts
1/2 cup (50 g) chopped almonds
1 onion

1 clove garlic
scant 1/2 cup (100 g) ricotta
1 bunch basil
3 tbsp (50 ml) extra virgin olive oil
chili pepper
salt, pepper

METHOD

Peel the tomatoes, remove the seeds, and coarsely chop.
Chop the onion and fry until golden in a pan with the oil and peeled clove of garlic, still whole.
Add the coarsely chopped almonds and pine nuts, cook for a couple of minutes, then add the chopped tomatoes and season with salt and pepper.
Season to taste with a little chili pepper.
Cook for about 15 minutes, then stir the ricotta into the sauce after removing the garlic. Lastly, add the chopped basil.
Cook the conchiglioni in plenty of salted boiling water until al dente; drain and dress with the pesto.

Preparation time: 30'
Cooking time: 12'

GARGANELLI
ALLA CRUDAIOLA

INGREDIENTS FOR **4** PEOPLE

12 oz (350 g) garganelli or other quill-shaped pasta
3 tbsp (50 ml) extra virgin olive oil
1 lb 2 oz (500 g) ribbed tomatoes
10 leaves fresh basil
1 clove garlic
salt and pepper

METHOD

Wash and dry the tomatoes, remove the seeds, then cut into thin strips.
Arrange in a large salad bowl and pour over the extra virgin olive oil.
Wash the basil, gently pat dry and tear into pieces. Peel the garlic and chop very finely.
Sprinkle the basil and garlic over the tomato slices.
Stir carefully and leave to marinate in a cool place for a couple of hours.
Meanwhile cook the garganelli in plenty of salted water until al dente,
drain carefully, then transfer into the bowl with the tomatoes.
Mix well before serving.

Preparation time: 10'
Resting time: 2 h - Cooking time: 9'

EGGPLANT GNOCCHI
WITH BONITO, CHERRY TOMATOES,
AND RED ONION FRITTERS

INGREDIENTS FOR 4 PEOPLE

FOR THE GNOCCHI
1lb 2oz (1 kg) eggplants
1 2/3 cups (200 g) all-purpose flour
1 2/3 cups (180 g) breadcrumbs
1 egg
2 tbsp (30 ml) olive oil

salt and pepper

FOR THE SAUCE
9 oz (250 g) bonito fillet
7 oz (200 g) Pachino tomatoes
1 clove garlic

5 oz (150 g) red onion
1 tsp thyme leaves
1/3 cup (80 ml) extra virgin olive oil
2/3 cup (80 g) all-purpose flour
1/2 cup + 1 tbsp (100 ml) milk
olive oil for frying

METHOD

Wash and peel the eggplants with a potato peeler. Put some of the skin aside and later chop it finely into matchsticks, then deep-fry to use as decoration. Cut the eggplant into slices about 1 in (2.5 cm) thick, sprinkle with salt and leave to stand for 20 minutes to remove excess moisture. Preheat the oven to 300°F (150°C) . Brush the eggplant slices evenly with extra virgin olive oil and bake for about 45 minutes.

When they are cooked, put the eggplant slices in a food processor and purée them until the mixture is smooth and even. Pour this purée into a container and leave to cool. Then stir in all the other ingredients listed for the gnocchi, kneading the dough very briskly. When the dough is ready, form it into long cylinders 3/4 in (2 cm) in diameter, then cut into pieces 3/4 in (2 cm) long. Cut the bonito flesh into cubes and fry in a pan together with the clove of garlic, peeled but left whole, and the thyme.

Meanwhile wash the cherry tomatoes, remove the seeds, and cut each one into quarters. Add to the bonito and cook for a couple more minutes, then remove from the heat. Chop the onion finely into thin strips and put in the milk to soak for a few minutes, then drain and coat in flour. Deep-fry in very hot oil until crisp. Cook the gnocchi in plenty of salted boiling water until they rise to the surface; then drain and pour the sauce over the top. Arrange in a dish and serve with the red onion fritters.

Preparation time: 1 h 16'
Cooking time: 6'

TOMATO
AND BREAD SOUP

INGREDIENTS FOR **4** PEOPLE

9 oz (500 g) ripe vine tomatoes
7 oz (200 g) onion
1 cup (250 ml) water
1 cup (20 g) basil leaves
3 cloves garlic

1/2 tsp chili pepper, powdered
about 1 lb (400-500 g) day-old baguette
scant 1/2 cup (100 ml) extra virgin olive oil
salt and pepper

METHOD

Wash the tomatoes. Make an X-shaped incision in the skin at one end of each one, then blanch them in boiling water for 10 to 15 seconds. Remove and peel, then cut into four quarters. Remove the seeds and push the tomato quarters through a sieve.
Heat 1/3 cup (80 ml) of the oil, add the coarsely chopped onions, the peeled clove of garlic, left whole (it will be removed at the end of the cooking). Add the powdered chili pepper. Simmer in the oil until soft.
Now add the puréed tomatoes and water, cover and simmer over low heat. Season with salt and pepper.
Cut the stale bread into cubes and toast in a non-stick pan without any fat added.
Wash and dry the basil, then tear into pieces. After the tomato mixture has cooked for about 25 to 30 minutes, add the bread and the basil. Cover and leave the bread to soften.
Sprinkle with a dash of olive oil before serving.

Preparation time: 10'
Cooking time: 30'

PENNE ALL'ARRABBIATA

INGREDIENTS FOR **4** PEOPLE

12 oz (350 g) penne
2 tbsp (30 ml) extra virgin olive oil
1 lb 2 oz (500 g) cherry tomatoes
2 cloves garlic
1 tsp chopped parsley (optional)
chili pepper
salt

METHOD

Peel and thinly slice the clove of garlic.
Heat the oil in a pan. Add the garlic and chili pepper to taste, making sure that the garlic does not brown too much.
If you are using fresh chili pepper, slice it finely first, but if you are using dried chili pepper, wear disposable gloves when you crumble it into the pan.
Wash and dry the tomatoes, then cut them in half. Add to the fried garlic and chili pepper. Season with salt and continue cooking over medium heat for about 15 minutes, stirring occasionally.
Meanwhile, boil the penne in plenty of salted boiling water until al dente.
Then drain them, put in a bowl and pour the sauce over the top.
Sprinkle with chopped parsley before serving.

Preparation time: 30'
Cooking time: 9'

PIZZA
ALLA NAPOLETANA

INGREDIENTS FOR **4** PEOPLE

FOR THE DOUGH
5 1/5 cups (650 g) soft wheat flour
or pizza flour
1 1/2 cups (375 ml) water
1 tsp (5 g) brewer's yeast
3 tsp (18 g) salt

FOR THE TOPPING
7 oz (200 g) tomato purée
14 oz (400 g) ribbed tomatoes
1 lb 2 oz (500 g) buffalo mozzarella
1/2 bunch fresh basil
salt
extra virgin olive oil

METHOD

Dissolve the yeast in a little warm water. On a pastry board knead the flour and water together with the yeast. Dissolve the salt in a little water and add it last. Cover the dough with plastic film and leave to rise in a warm place until doubled in volume: this will take from 1 to 4 hours, depending on the room temperature. Divide the dough into four portions and shape each portion into a ball. Cover again with plastic film, put in a warm place and leave to rise once more until it has doubled in volume (this will take between 30 and 90 minutes, depending on the temperature of the room).
Coat the pastry board generously with flour and flatten the balls of dough with your hands, starting with the tip of your fingers before continuing with rotating movement of your hands. Slice or dice the tomatoes. Add a pinch of salt and a drop of olive oil to the tomato purée. Spread this mixture over the pizzas and garnish with the sliced or diced tomatoes. Drain the buffalo mozzarella thoroughly and crumble it over the top. Preheat the oven to 480°F (250° C). Put the pizzas on a baking sheet and bake for about 8 minutes. Remove from the oven and decorate with fresh basil leaves, carefully washed and dried.

Preparation time: 30'
Rising time: 1 h 30' – 5 h 30' - Cooking time: 8'

TOMATO
RISOTTO

INGREDIENTS FOR **4** PEOPLE

1 lb 2 oz (500 g) vine tomatoes
1 tbsp (15 ml) extra virgin olive oil
10 oz (300 g) Vialone nano rice
1 small onion
scant 1/2 cup (100 ml) dry white wine

6 1/3 cups (1.5 liters) vegetable stock
1/4 cup (60 g) butter
3/4 cup (80 g) grated Parmesan
salt

METHOD

Peel the tomatoes, remove the seeds, cut half of them into dice and put to one side.
Chop the onion and put one-third of it in a small frying pan with one-third of the oil. Fry until golden,
then add the tomatoes, season with salt and cook for 10 minutes over high heat.
When the tomato-onion mixture has finished cooking, put in a blender and purée. Keep it warm.
Meanwhile in another pan, soften the remaining chopped onion in 4 tsp (20 g) butter. Add the rice and stir it
in the mixture. Now pour in the wine and cook gently until it has evaporated completely, stirring all the time.
Continue cooking, adding half the puréed tomato mixture and pouring in the stock a little at a time,
stirring continuously. After about 10 minutes, add the diced tomatoes.
When the rice-tomato mixture is cooked, check the seasoning. Remove from the heat and
fold in the rest of the butter and the grated Parmesan.
Garnish with the rest of the sauce.

Preparation time: 30'
Cooking time: 16-18'

SPAGHETTI
WITH TOMATO SAUCE

INGREDIENTS FOR **4** PEOPLE

2 1/4 lb (1 kg) vine tomatoes
12 oz (350 g) spaghetti
2 tbsp (30 ml) extra virgin olive oil
1 onion or scallion
1 clove garlic
1 tsp chopped parsley (optional)
salt and pepper

METHOD

Peel the tomatoes and remove the seeds, then cut them into 3/8-in (1-cm) cubes.
In a pan, fry the chopped onion or shallot in the oil until golden, together with the peeled clove of garlic,
still whole. When the onion has turned a beautiful golden color, add the cubed tomatoes, then season with
salt and pepper. Cook the sauce over medium heat for about 10 minutes, stirring occasionally.
When the sauce is cooked, remove the garlic clove.
Cook the spaghetti in salted boiling water. Cook until al dente, drain carefully
and pour the tomato sauce over it.
Optionally, garnish with a little chopped parsley.

Preparation time: 30'
Cooking time: 8'

SPAGHETTI WITH MARINATED CHERRY TOMATOES AND RICOTTA

INGREDIENTS FOR **4** PEOPLE

12 oz (350 g) spaghetti
3 tbsp (50 ml) extra virgin olive oil
10 oz (300 g) grape tomatoes
1 clove garlic
1 bunch basil
2/3 cup (150 g) ricotta

1/3 cup (30 g) grated Pecorino
mint
chives
thyme
parsley
salt and pepper

METHOD

Wash and carefully dry the herbs, then chop them finely and put in a bowl. Wash and dry the cherry tomatoes and cut into four quarters. Peel and crush the clove of garlic, then add the tomatoes and garlic to the chopped herbs. Add plenty of oil and season with salt and pepper.
Leave to marinate for at least 30 minutes.
Cook the spaghetti in salted boiling water until al dente, then drain, reserving a little of the cooking water to stir into the ricotta.
Sauté the pasta in a pan with the marinated cherry tomatoes and the ricotta.
Sprinkle with grated Pecorino before serving.

Preparation time: 40'
Cooking time: 8'

TAGLIATELLE
WITH BOLOGNESE SAUCE

INGREDIENTS FOR 4 PEOPLE

FOR THE TAGLIATELLE
2 1/2 cups (300 g) all-purpose flour
3 eggs

FOR THE SAUCE
2/3 cup (160 ml) water
6 oz (150 g) ground pork shoulder

5 oz (150 g) ground beef
5 oz (150 g) lard
1 1/2 oz (40 g) carrot (1 small)
1 1/2 oz (40 g) celery (2 small stalks)
1 1/2 oz (40 g) yellow onion (1/2 small)
1 lb 2 oz (500 g) Piccadilly tomatoes

1 tbsp (20 g) tomato paste
1/3 cup (40 g) grated Parmesan
1/3 cup (100 ml) red wine
100 ml extra virgin olive oil
2 bay leaves
black pepper, salt

64

METHOD

Mix the flour with the eggs until you have a smooth, even mixture. Wrap the mixture in plastic film and leave
to rest in the refrigerator for 30 minutes. Then remove from the refrigerator and, with a rolling pin, roll out
the pasta dough to a thickness of a U.S. penny (1 mm). Now cut strips about 1/4-in (6 mm) wide: the tagliatelle.
Spread them onto a lightly floured work surface. Chop the vegetables, previously washed and dried.
Add the oil to a medium-sized pan and add the chopped bacon fat and vegetables
together with the bay leaves shredded by hand, and fry over medium heat.
When all the ingredients have turned golden, add the ground meat and fry briskly over high heat.
Add the red wine and continue cooking until all the liquid has evaporated.
Then lower the heat and add the chopped tomatoes and the tomato concentrate. Season with salt
and pepper. Continue cooking over low heat for about an hour, adding a little water if necessary.
Boil the tagliatelle in plenty of salted boiling water until al dente,
then drain and transfer into a bowl with the sauce.
Sprinkle with grated Parmesan, stir well and serve.

Preparation time: 1 h 30'
Cooking time: 3-4'

TOMATO SOUP

INGREDIENTS FOR 4 PEOPLE

2 1/4 lb (1 kg) vine tomatoes
3 1/2 oz (100 g) onion (1 1/2 small)
1 cup (20 g) basil
1 clove garlic
7 oz (200 g) day-old bread
generous 1/3 cup (100 ml) extra virgin olive oil
salt and pepper

METHOD

Wash the tomatoes. Make an X-shaped incision in the skin at one end of each one, then blanch them in boiling water for 10 to 15 seconds. Remove and peel, then cut into four quarters. Remove the seeds and push the tomato quarters through a sieve.
Wash and dry the basil. Chop up the onion coarsely and soften in a pan with a little oil together with the clove of garlic, peeled but left whole (it will be removed at the end). Add the tomato purée you have made and simmer on low heat. Season with salt and pepper and the basil.
Cut the bread into slices and toast in non-stick pan without any oil or fat added.
Liquidize in a blender and serve with the bread crostini.

Preparation time: 10'
Cooking time: 30'

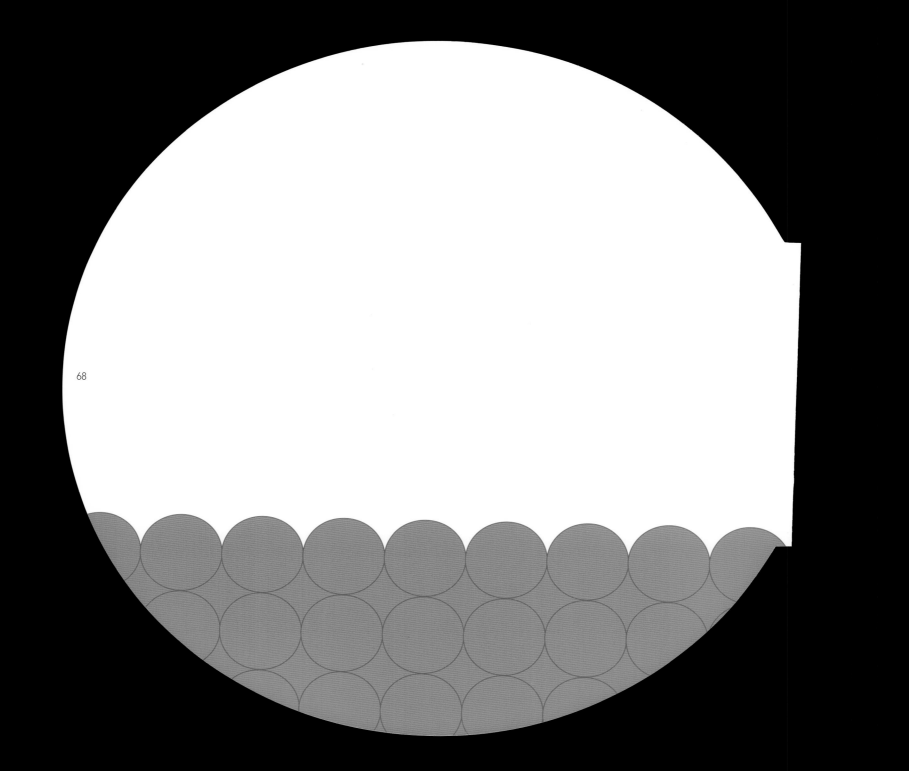

68

Second Courses

ANCHOVIES WITH TOMATOES, CAPERS, AND TAGGIASCA OLIVES

INGREDIENTS FOR 4 PEOPLE

1 3/4 lb (800 g) fresh anchovies
3 oz (80 g) Taggiasca olives
1 oz (30 g) salted anchovies
7 oz (200 g) San Marzano tomatoes
1 tbsp (10 g) capers, well rinsed

1/4 cup + 2 tsp (70 ml) white wine
1 clove garlic
1/2 cup (30 g) chopped parsley
2 tbsp (30 ml) extra virgin olive oil
salt

METHOD

Clean the anchovies, remove the bones, and open out the fish like a book. Wash and chop the tomatoes. Wash, dry, and chop the parsley. Finely chop the garlic. Heat the oil in a pan, then add the garlic and parsley. Fry until transparent but not colored. Add the white wine and, when it has evaporated, add the chopped tomatoes. Meanwhile rinse the salt off the salted anchovies, remove the bones and chop coarsely. Then add them and the capers to the pan. Cook for a few minutes. Finally add the fresh anchovies and Taggiasca olives. Continue cooking for a few more minutes. Season with a pinch of salt and serve.

Preparation time: 20'
Cooking time: 15'

VEAL ESCALOPES
NEAPOLITAN STYLE

INGREDIENTS FOR **4** PEOPLE

8 veal escalopes. 2 oz (60 g each)
1 1/4 cups (120 g) grated Pecorino
2/5 cup (50 g) all-purpose flour
1 tsp chopped parsley
3 tbsp (40 ml) extra virgin olive oil
1 lb 2 oz (500 g) grape tomatoes
salt and pepper

METHOD

Heat half the oil in a pan. Wash the tomatoes and cut in half, then add to the hot oil in the pan.
Cook for 20 minutes, adding a spoonful of water if necessary. Season with salt and pepper.
Meanwhile, beat the escalopes to flatten them. Sprinkle the grated Pecorino and parsley over them,
then roll up in the shape of a roulade. Secure the rolls with some string or a toothpick.
Coat the roulades lightly in flour and fry in the pan with the rest of the oil for a few minutes.
Season with salt and pepper.
Drain and place in the pan with the tomato sauce.
Continue cooking for a few more minutes.

Preparation time: 20'
Cooking time: 30'

MUSSELS
ALLA MARINARA

INGREDIENTS FOR 4 PEOPLE

2 1/4 lb (1 kg) mussels
1 clove garlic
4 tbsp (60 ml) extra virgin olive oil
2/5 cup (100 ml) white wine
7 oz (200 g) Piccadilly tomatoes
7 oz (200 g) baguette
parsley
chili pepper
salt

METHOD

Heat the oil in a large pan. Peel and chop the clove of garlic. Wash, dry, and chop the parsley.
Add both to the pan with the chili pepper and fry until transparent but without coloring.
Add the white wine and cook until it evaporates. Meanwhile peel the tomatoes,
remove the seeds, cut into small dice, then add to the pan.
Carefully clean mussels and cook until they open.
Sprinkle with dash of extra virgin olive oil before serving.
Serve with the baguette, sliced and toasted in the oven or on a grill.

Preparation time: 20'
Cooking time: 5'

FILLET OF SEA BASS WITH CHERRY TOMATOES, CAPERS, AND OLIVES

INGREDIENTS FOR **4** PEOPLE

1lb 2 oz (500 g) sea bass
4 tbsp (60 ml) extra virgin olive oil
3 1/2 oz (100 g) green olives (about 36)
7 oz (200 g) cherry tomatoes
2 tbsp (20 g) capers
parsley
salt and pepper

METHOD

Clean the sea bass, remove the skin, then wash and fillet it.
Put the fillets in a lightly oiled pan. Wash and dry the tomatoes, cut them in half,
and add to the pan. Season with salt and pepper.
Rinse the capers in water and add to the pan. Sprinkle the remaining oil over the pan before covering it,
then cook for 15 minutes over low heat or in a moderate oven, adding a little water if necessary.
Towards the end of the cooking time, add the olives and sprinkle a little chopped parsley on top.

Preparation time: 20'
Cooking time: 15'

MILLE FEUILLE OF SCAMPI WITH CANDIED TOMATOES AND BASIL-FLAVORED OIL

INGREDIENTS FOR **4** PEOPLE

16 scampi
1 1/4 cups (30 g) fresh basil leaves
3 1/2 oz (100 g) mixed salad
3 tbsp (40 ml) extra virgin olive oil

FOR THE CANDIED TOMATOES
2 1/2 lb (1.2 kg) ripe vine tomatoes

1 clove garlic
1/4 cup (10 g) thyme
2 tsp (10 ml) extra virgin olive oil
sugar
salt and pepper

METHOD

Remove the shells from the scampi. Season with salt, pepper, and some of the oil, then leave to marinate. Wash and dry the tomatoes, plunge in boiling water for half a minute, the place in water and ice to cool rapidly. Cut each into four quarters and remove the seeds. Place on a baking sheet lined with parchment paper. Sprinkle with the thyme leaves, sliced garlic clove and a pinch of salt, pepper, and sugar. Preheat the oven to 175° F (80°C). Bake for one hour.
Line another baking sheet with parchment paper and place four square pastry cutters or cookie cutters on it. Fill the molds with alternate layers of tomatoes and scampi. Finish with a layer of tomatoes Preheat the oven to 300°F (150°C). Place the molds in the oven and bake for 6 minutes.
Meanwhile blanch the basil leaves in a little boiling water for a couple of minutes, then drain and put immediately in water and ice. Drain them and purée with the rest of the oil, using a hand-held mixer. Remove the molds from the oven and serve the mille feuille with a mixed salad and the basil oil.

Preparation time: 1 h 36'
Cooking time: 6'

DOGFISH
ALLA LIVORNESE

INGREDIENTS FOR 4 PEOPLE

1 lb 2 oz (500 g) vine tomatoes
1 3/4 lb (800 g) dogfish in slices
1 onion
1 clove garlic
4 tbsp (60 ml) extra virgin olive oil
2/5 cup (100 ml) white wine
parsley
salt and pepper

METHOD

Heat the oil in a pan. Chop the onion and the peeled clove of garlic.
Add to the pan and fry until transparent but without coloring.
Add the slices of dogfish and fry on both sides.
Add the white wine and cook to evaporate. Meanwhile peel the tomatoes and remove the seeds.
Cut into small dice, then add to the pan. Cook for about 15 minutes.
Season with salt and pepper, adding a little water if necessary.
Wash, dry, and chop the parsley. Sprinkle into the sauce towards the end of the cooking time.

Preparation time: 20'
Cooking time: 15'

CHICKEN ALLA CACCIATORE

INGREDIENTS FOR 4 PEOPLE

2 1/4 lb (1 kg) vine tomatoes
1 chicken
generous 1/3 cup (100 ml)
extra virgin olive oil
3/4 cup + 1 1/2 tbsp (200 ml) white wine
1 onion
1 carrot

1 stick celery
1 clove garlic
1 bay leaf
1 sprig rosemary
1 sprig sage
flour, stock
salt and pepper

METHOD

Cut the chicken into 4 or 8 portions, depending on your choice.
Season with salt and pepper and fry lightly in a pan with oil.
Cut into thin strips. Put a little oil in a second pan. Add the vegetable
strips with the rosemary, bay leaves, and sage tied together, and the peeled clove of garlic, still whole.
Wash the onion, carrot, and celery. Cut into thin strips.
Fry all together until golden.
Add the sautéed chicken portions and stir in the white wine.
Wash the tomatoes and remove the seeds, then chop into small pieces.
Cook until the wine has evaporated, then add the chopped tomatoes.
Continue cooking for about 30 minutes, adding enough stock to end up with a fairly thick sauce.
Add more stock if it has evaporated too much. When cooked, remove the bundle of herbs.
Serve the chicken with plenty of sauce.

Preparation time: 30'
Cooking time: 30'

VEAL ESCALOPES ALLA PIZZAIOLA

INGREDIENTS FOR **4** PEOPLE

1 lb 2 oz (500 g) Piccadilly
tomatoes
8 veal escalopes
of about 2 oz (60 g) each
4 tbsp (60 ml) extra virgin olive oil

4 1/2 tbsp (40 g) capers
8 slices sandwich loaf (optional)
flour
oregano
salt

METHOD

Cut the crusts off the slices of a sandwich loaf and toast them in the oven
or on the grill, if you intend to use them as base for the escalopes.
Trim the escalopes and beat them lightly.
Wash and dry the tomatoes and cut them into cubes.
Heat the oil in a pan, add the escalopes, lightly coated in flour, and fry them briskly on both sides.
Season with salt and keep in a warm place.
In the same pan, add the tomatoes and cook over high heat for 5 minutes. Adjust the seasoning,
adding a little salt if necessary, as well as a little oregano and the rinsed capers.
Return the escalopes to the pan and finish cooking quickly.
Optionally, serve on crostini.

Preparation time: 30'

EGGS
WITH TOMATOES

INGREDIENTS FOR 4 PEOPLE

1 1/2 lb (600 g) ribbed tomatoes
4 eggs
3 tbsp (50 ml) extra virgin olive oil
1 small bunch chives
salt

METHOD

Wash and dry the tomatoes, remove the remains of the stalks and cut into 3/8-in (1-cm) cubes.
Heat half the oil in a pan, add the tomatoes, season with salt, and fry briskly over high heat for 1 to 2 minutes.
Meanwhile heat the rest of the oil in another pan. Place round rings or cookie cutters in the pan and break
the eggs very carefully into them. Cook over moderate heat until the whites have set.
Sprinkle salt only on the whites.
Using a clean ring as a guide, put the tomatoes on the plates and place the eggs on top with a spatula.
Garnish with washed and dried lengths of chives.

Preparation time: 10'
Cooking time: 5'

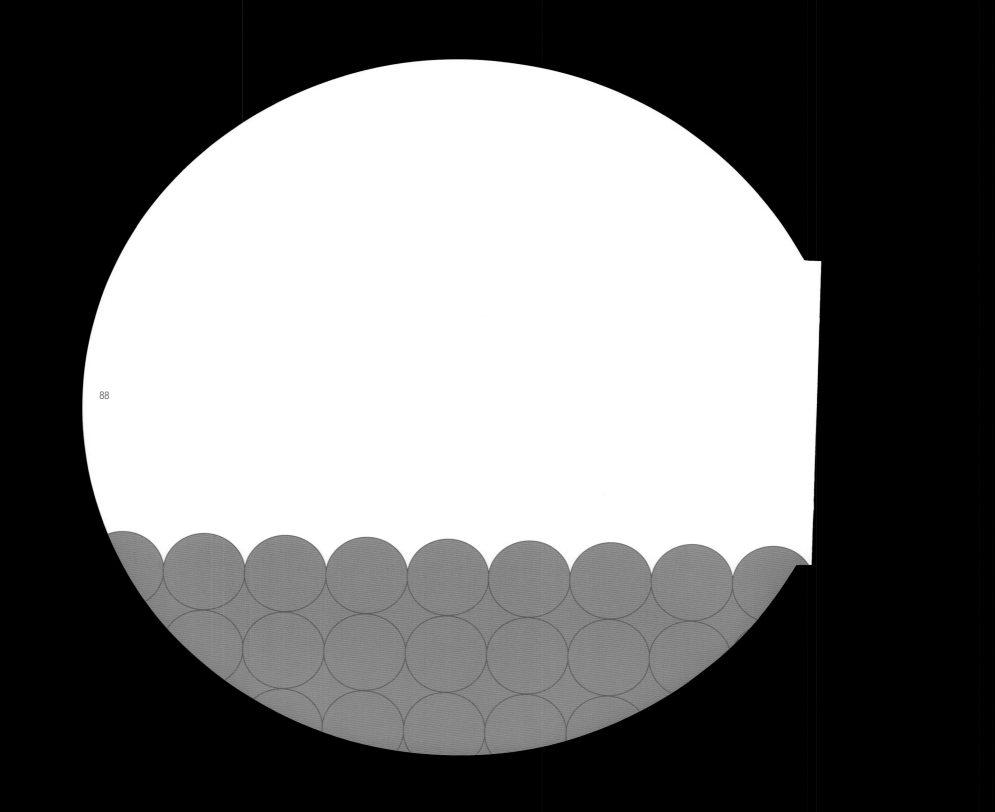

88

Vegetable Dishes

CANNELLINI BEAN STEW

INGREDIENTS FOR **4** PEOPLE

7 oz (200 g) cannellini beans
7 oz (200 g) tomatoes
2 tbsp (30 ml) extra virgin olive oil
1 clove garlic
1 tbsp chopped parsley
1 sprig thyme
salt and pepper

METHOD

Soak the cannellini beans in cold water for 12 hours. Then drain them and cook in
unsalted boiling water for 15 to 20 minutes.
Meanwhile, peel the tomatoes and remove the seeds, then cut into cubes.
Wash and dry the parsley and thyme. Chop the parsley and garlic. Heat the oil in a pan, add
the parsley, garlic, and the whole sprig of thyme. Drain the cooked cannellini beans just a little,
then add together with the cubed tomatoes. Season with a little salt and pepper
and continue cooking for a few more minutes.
Serve with ground black pepper.

Soaking time: 12 h
Preparation time: 15' - Cooking time: 40'

VEGETARIAN MILLE FEUILLE

INGREDIENTS FOR **4** PEOPLE

10 oz (300 g) salad tomatoes
7 oz (200 g) yellow bell peppers
5 oz (150 g) grated celery
7 oz (200 g) squash
5 oz (150 g) radicchio
7 oz (200 g) fennel
9 oz (250 g) zucchini
6 eggplants

7 oz (200 g) red onions
7 oz (200 g) leeks
generous 1/3 cup (100 ml) milk
3 tbsp (50 ml) extra virgin olive oil
flour
oil for frying
salt and pepper

METHOD

Clean and wash all the vegetables. Cut the white parts of the leeks into thin strips, leave to soak for 10 minutes in the milk, then drain thoroughly. Coat in flour and deep-fry in plenty of boiling oil. Drain and leave to dry on a paper towel, season with salt, and put to one side.
Cook the peppers in the oven or grill them, then peel them and cut across their length into round slices. Cut the eggplant, onion, and zucchini into discs about 1/8-in (3 mm) thick. Slice the celeriac and squash, then cut them into discs the same size as the other vegetables, using a pastry cutter. Cut the fennel and radicchio into slices. Cook the celeriac for 5 minutes in salted boiling water with some lemon juice added. In another pan, parboil the pumpkin for one minute. Cook the eggplant, onion, zucchini, celeriac, squash, fennel, and radicchio on the grill, or bake in the oven with a dash of extra virgin olive oil. Season all the vegetables with salt and pepper and a dash of oil. Leave to marinate in a bowl for at least 15 minutes. Make the mille feuille by placing the various vegetables on top of each other in layers. Garnish with the deep-fried leeks.

Preparation time: 45'

PANZANELLA

INGREDIENTS FOR 4/6 PEOPLE

2 1/4 lb (1 kg) day-old bread
1 oz (30 g) anchovy fillets
7 oz (200 g) vine tomatoes
4 oz (120 g) cucumber (without seeds)
5 oz (150 g) red onions
9 oz (250 g) bell peppers

1 clove garlic, chopped
1 tbsp capers, well rinsed
1 bunch basil
1 tbsp (15 ml) red wine vinegar
1/3 cup (80 ml) extra virgin olive oil
1/2 tsp (3 g) salt
black pepper

METHOD

Cut the bread into cubes of about 3/4 in (2 cm), leaving the crusts on.
Cut the tomatoes into cubes of the same size.
Peel and chop up garlic with the anchovies and capers and place in a large bowl.
Add the salt, ground black pepper, vinegar, and oil, and stir well.
Meanwhile, wash and dry all the other vegetables and cut them into cubes. Add to the bowl
together with bread. Mix well and add more salt and pepper if necessary.

CHEF'S TIP

The panzanella will be even tastier and more delicious if prepared the day before
and left in the refrigerator overnight to allow the flavors to develop.

Preparation time: 15'

PEPERONATA

1 lb 2 oz (500 g) San Marzano tomatoes
1 lb 2 oz (500 g) bell peppers
3 1/2 oz (100 g) onion
1 tbsp (10 g) capers
1 clove garlic
3 tbsp (50 ml) extra virgin olive oil
salt and pepper

METHOD

Cut the onion into slices and fry in a pan with the oil, the chopped capers,
and the peeled clove of garlic, still whole.
Wash and dry the peppers, cut into large pieces, then add to the onion-capers mixture in the pan.
Season with salt and pepper. Cook for about 15 minutes.
Meanwhile wash and dry the tomatoes. Cut into slices, add to the pan,
and continue cooking for another 15 minutes.

Preparation time: 15'
Cooking time: 30'

TOMATOES
MEDITERRANEAN STYLE

INGREDIENTS FOR **4** PEOPLE

1 lb 2 oz (500 g) vine tomatoes
1 1/4 cups (125 g) breadcrumbs
4 tbsp (60 ml) extra virgin olive oil
1 tsp chopped parsley
1 tsp chopped basil
1/2 tsp thyme leaves
1/2 tsp oregano
1/2 tsp chopped marjoram
salt

METHOD

Wash the tomatoes, remove the stalks, then cut into half.
Sprinkle with salt and leave to drain for about 15 minutes.
Meanwhile, wash and dry all the herbs and finely chop them.
Stir into the breadcrumbs, add the extra virgin olive oil and mix well
Preheat the oven to 350°F (180°C). Spread the mixture on the tomato halves
and bake for about 15 minutes.

Preparation time: 20'
Cooking time: 15'

TOMATOES WITH CAPONATA

INGREDIENTS FOR **4** PEOPLE

1 lb 2 oz (500 g) ribbed tomatoes
2/5 cup (100 ml)
extra virgin olive oil
1 clove garlic
1 eggplant
3 1/2 oz (100 g) zucchini
2 oz (50 g) celery
2 oz (50 g) red onion

2 tbsp (20 g) capers
2 tbsp (15 g) pine nuts
2 tbsp (15 g) pistachio nuts, shelled
1 bunch basil
1 tbsp (10 g) sugar
1 tbsp vinegar
thyme
salt and pepper

METHOD

Clean and wash all the vegetables.
Cut one tomato into slices about 1/4 in (6 mm) thick and cook briefly on the grill.
Remove the seeds from the remaining tomatoes and cut into small cubes. Cut the eggplant into
small cubes as well. Sprinkle with a little salt and leave to drain.
Then fry in olive oil.
Dice the onion, celery, and zucchini. Fry the onion and celery in a little oil until golden.
Add the zucchini and sauté lightly. Add the capers and pine nuts. Stir in the diced eggplant and tomatoes.
Season with salt and pepper and cook on a low heat for about 20 minutes.
Towards the end of the cooking time add the vinegar and sugar, followed by a few pistachio nuts.
Serve the caponata on the sliced tomatoes cooked on the grill earlier.

Preparation time: 30'

BAKED STUFFED TOMATOES

INGREDIENTS FOR 4 PEOPLE

3 1/2 oz (100 g) ground beef
1/2 cup (50 g) grated Parmesan
2 eggs
2 1/2 tbsp (50 g) breadcrumbs

4 vine tomatoes
3 tbsp (50 ml) extra virgin olive oil
nutmeg
salt and pepper

METHOD

Wash the tomatoes and cut off the upper part. Remove the seeds and liquid, preserving the pulp.
In a pan heat three-quarters of the oil listed in the recipe. Add the minced beef and brown it, then add the
tomato pulp. Cook for a few minutes to evaporate the excess liquid, then season with salt and pepper.
Transfer everything to a bowl and let it cool a little. Then add the eggs, the grated Parmesan
(reserving a tablespoonful for finishing the dish before baking), and the breadcrumbs.
Check the seasoning and add some grated nutmeg.
With a spoon or a pastry bag, fill the tomatoes with this mixture. Arrange them on a baking sheet
greased with a little oil. Sprinkle with the remaining Parmesan and a drop of oil.
Bake at 350°F (180°C) for about 30 minutes.
Serve the stuffed tomatoes hot from the oven or cold according to taste.

Preparation time: 30'
Cooking time: 30'

RATATOUILLE

INGREDIENTS FOR 4 PEOPLE

7 oz (200 g) eggplants
10 oz (300 g) zucchini
7 oz (200 g) grape tomatoes
6 oz (180 g) red onion
3 1/2 oz (100 g) red bell peppers

3 1/2 oz (100 g) yellow bell peppers
1 clove garlic. 4 leaves basil
generous 1/3 cup (100 ml)
extra virgin olive oil
salt and pepper

METHOD

Wash and dry the eggplants, zucchinis, and peppers. Cut into 3/4-in (2-cm) cubes.
Wash the tomatoes and cut in half. Peel the onions and slice.
Heat the oil in a pan over medium heat and add the peeled clove of garlic, left whole, and the onion.
Fry until softened. Now add the peppers, then after a few minutes the eggplant, and a little later the
zucchini. Fry for a few minutes, then add the tomatoes and season with salt and pepper.
Continue cooking over a low heat. Meanwhile wash and dry the basil leaves, tear into pieces,
and add to the tomato mixture.

Preparation time: 10'
Cooking time: 20'

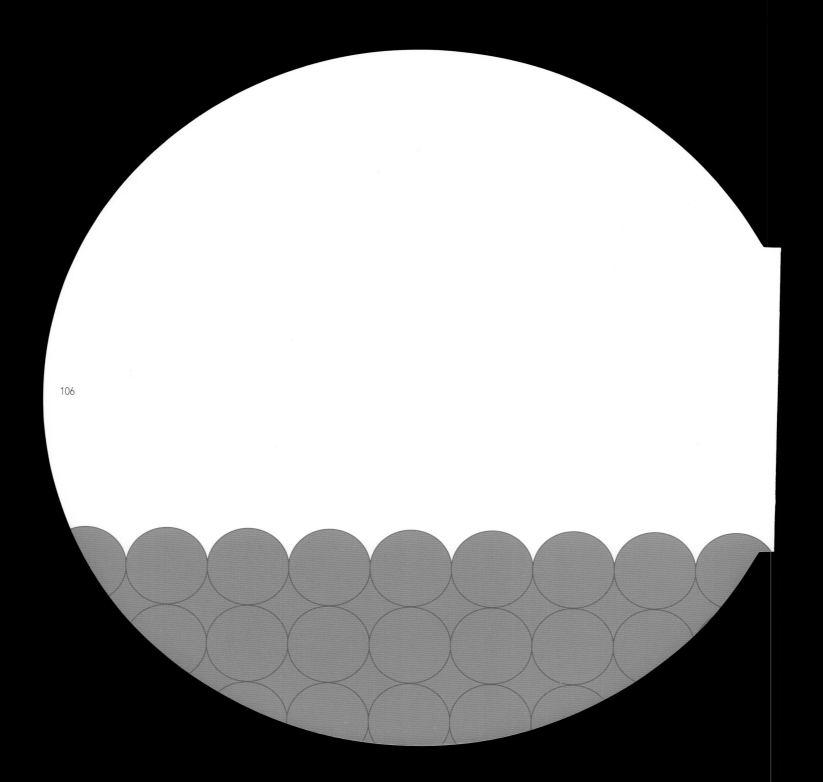

106

Preserves, Sauces, and Desserts

BAGNETTO ROSSO: SAVORY RED SAUCE

INGREDIENTS FOR 4 PEOPLE

1 lb 2 oz (1 kg) cherry tomatoes
1 tbsp (20 g) tomato paste
5 oz (150 g) onion
3 1/2 oz (100 g) carrot
2 1/2 oz (70 g) celery
2 oz (50 g) bell peppers

2 cloves garlic
1 tsp chopped parsley
1 bunch basil
2 tbsp (30 ml) extra virgin olive oil
salt and pepper
chili pepper

METHOD

Peel the cherry tomatoes and remove the seeds, then cut into four quarters.
Chop the onion, carrot, celery, pepper, and garlic and gently fry in a pan with a little oil until golden.
When they have softened, add the parsley, basil, and chili pepper.
After a couple of minutes, add the cherry tomatoes and tomato purée, then season with salt and pepper.
Cook over low heat for about 2 hours, stirring occasionally.
At the end, adjust the seasoning, adding a little salt and chili pepper if necessary.

Preparation time: 15'
Cooking time: 2 h

TOMATO CARAMELS

INGREDIENTS FOR 4 PEOPLE

1 lb 2 oz (500 g) vine tomatoes
scant 1/2 cup (85 g) sugar
3 tsp (10 g) agar-agar or powdered gelatin

METHOD

Peel the tomatoes, remove the seeds, then purée in a blender.
Mix the sugar with the agar-agar or gelatin, then stir into the puréed tomatoes.
Pour the mixture into a pan and bring to the boil, stirring all the time.
Continue boiling for one or two minutes.
Then pour this mixture into molds or a high-sided baking tray.
Leave to cool for about an hour.
When the mixture has cooled, cut into cubes or other shapes of your choice.

Preparation time: 30'
Cooking time: 2' - Resting time: 1 h

GREEN TOMATO CHUTNEY

INGREDIENTS FOR **4** PEOPLE

1 lb 2 oz (500 g) green tomatoes
5 oz (150 g) cane sugar
1 lemon

METHOD

Wash and dry the tomatoes, remove the seeds and cut into strips a about 1/4 in (6 mm) wide.
Put in a glass bowl together with the sugar, cover with plastic film and leave to stand until the following day.
The next day, wash the lemon, remove the zest, and squeeze the juice. Pour the tomato mixture into a pan.
Add the lemon juice and grated lemon zest. Cook for about 45 minutes, stirring frequently,
until the mixture has the consistency of thick jam.
Preheat the oven to 200°F (100°C). Put the glass preserving jars you will be using in the oven for 15 minutes.
Remove them and immediately pour in the tomato chutney mixture.
Seal the jars immediately and turn them upside down so that they form the vacuum necessary
to increase the food's keeping qualities.
Leave the jars upside down until completely cool, then store in a cool place.

Preparation time: 15'
Resting time: 12 h - Cooking time: 45'

TOMATOES IN A JAR

INGREDIENTS FOR ABOUT 1 1/2 LB (800 G) OF PRODUCT

2 1/4 lb (1 kg) San Marzano tomatoes
basil
salt

METHOD

Wash the tomatoes, make an X-shaped cut in the end with a small knife, then dip the tomatoes for
30 seconds in a pan filled with boiling water. Remove with a skimming ladle to drain them, then
leave to cool in a bowl of water and ice; this will make it easier to peel them.
Peel the tomatoes, cut in half, sprinkle with salt and leave to drain.
Cut the tomatoes into cubes. Wash and carefully dry the basil.
Put the cubed tomatoes and basil in glass preserving jars and seal them.
Wrap the jars in dish towels to prevent them breaking, arrange them in a large saucepan, cover with water,
and bring to the boil. Continue boiling over low heat for 20 minutes.
Let the jars cool in the sterilizing water, then check that they are properly sealed.
Store the jars of preserved tomatoes in a cool, dark place.

Preparation time: 1 h

DRIED TOMATOES IN OIL

INGREDIENTS FOR **4** PEOPLE

10 oz (300 g) dried tomatoes
3/4 cup + 1 1/2 tbsp (200 ml) water
3/4 cup + 1 1/2 tbsp (200 ml) white wine
2/5 cup (100 ml) wine vinegar
4 tsp (15 g) sugar
1 bay leaf
1 tsp ground pepper
1 tsp ground coriander
3 tsp (20 g) salt
extra virgin olive oil

METHOD

Put all the ingredients except the tomatoes and oil in a pan. Bring to the boil and,
when it is boiling, add the tomatoes. Simmer for 5 minutes. Once this has been done,
drain the tomatoes, dry with a cloth, and put them in glass preserving jars.
Cover with extra-virgin olive oil and seal the jars.
Store them in a cool, dark place.

Preparation time: 20'
Cooking time: 5'

BOTTLED
TOMATO SAUCE

INGREDIENTS TO MAKE ABOUT 1 LB 10 OZ (750 G) SAUCE

2 1/4 lb (1 kg) San Marzano
tomatoes

METHOD

Wash the tomatoes, make an X-shaped cut in the end with a small knife, then dip the tomatoes for
30 seconds in a pan filled with boiling water. Remove with a skimming ladle to drain them, then leave
to cool in a bowl of water and ice; this will make it easier to peel them.
Put through a sieve (or use a special machine) to remove the skins and seeds.
Fill the bottles and seal them.
Wrap the jars in dish towels to prevent them breaking, arrange them in a large saucepan,
cover with water, and bring to the boil. Continue boiling over low heat for 20 minutes.
Let the bottles cool in the sterilizing water, then check that they are properly sealed.
Store the bottles of tomato sauce in cool, dark place.

Preparation time: 1 h

TOMATO SORBET

INGREDIENTS TO MAKE ABOUT 3 CUPS (800 ML) OF SORBET

10 oz (300 g) grape tomatoes
3/4 cup + 1 1/2 tbsp (200 ml) water
3/4 cup (145 g) sugar
3 tbsp (40 g) dextrose
1/2 tsp (3.5 g) sorbet stabilizer
basil
salt and pepper

METHOD

Wash and dry the tomatoes, then purée them in a blender with the basil, salt and pepper.
Then push through a sieve.
Mix them together with all the other ingredients in a bowl.
Leave the mixture in the refrigerator to stand for at least 30 minutes,
then put in an ice cream machine and place in the freezer.

Preparation time: 30'

ALPHABETICAL INDEX OF RECIPES

123

ALPHABETICAL INDEX OF INGREDIENTS

ACADEMIA BARILLA
AMBASSADOR OF ITALIAN
GASTRONOMY THROUGHOUT THE WORLD

In the heart of Parma, one of the most distinguished capitals of Italian cuisine, is the Barilla Center. Set in the grounds of the former Barilla pasta factory, this modern architectural complex is the home of Academia Barilla. This was founded in 2004 to promote the art of Italian cuisine, protecting the regional gastronomic heritage and safeguarding it from imitations and counterfeits, while encouraging the great traditions of the Italian restaurant industry. Academia Barilla is also a center of great professionalism and talent that is exceptional in the world of cooking. It organizes cooking classes for culinary enthusiasts, it provides services for those involved in the restaurant industry, and it offers products of the highest quality. In 2007, Academia Barilla was awarded the "Premio Impresa-Cultura" for its campaigns promoting the culture and creativity of Italian gastronomy throughout the world. The center was designed to meet the training requirements of the world of food and it is equipped with all the multimedia facilities necessary for organizing major events. The remarkable gastronomic auditorium is surrounded by a restaurant, a laboratory for sensory analysis, and various teaching rooms equipped with the most modern technology. The Gastronomic Library contains over 10,000 books and a remarkable collection of historic menus as well as prints related to culinary subjects. The vast cultural heritage of the library can be consulted on the internet which provides access to hundreds of digitized historic texts.

This avant-garde approach and the presence of a team of internationally famous experts enables Academia Barilla to offer a wide range of courses, meeting the needs of both restaurant chefs and amateur food lovers. In addition, Academia Barilla arranges cultural events and activities aiming to develop the art of cooking, supervised by experts, chefs, and food critics, that are open to the public. It also organizes the "Academia Barilla Film Award", for short films devoted to Italy's culinary traditions.

www.academiabarilla.com

WHITE STAR PUBLISHERS

WS White Star Publishers® is a registered trademark
property of De Agostini Libri S.p.A.

© 2012 De Agostini Libri S.p.A.
Via G. da Verrazano, 15
28100 Novara, Italy
www.whitestar.it - www.deagostini.it

Translation and Editing: Rosetta Translations SARL

ISBN 978-88-544-0671-1
2 3 4 5 6   17 16 15 14 13

Printed in China

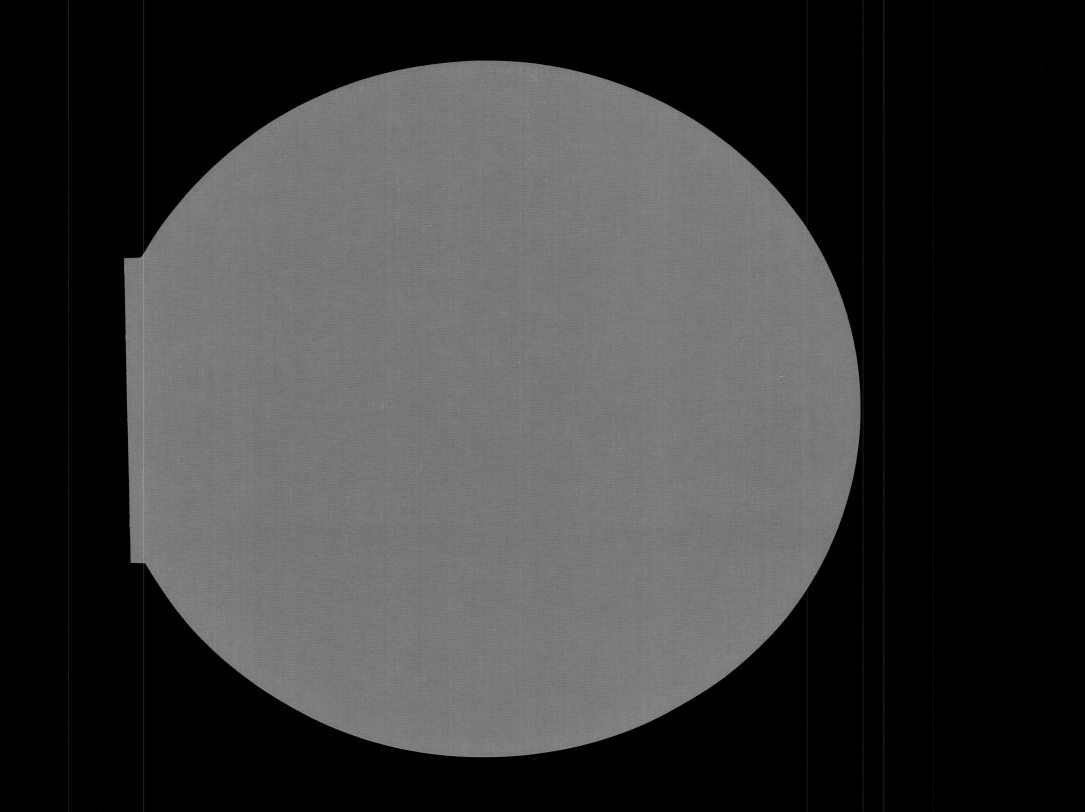

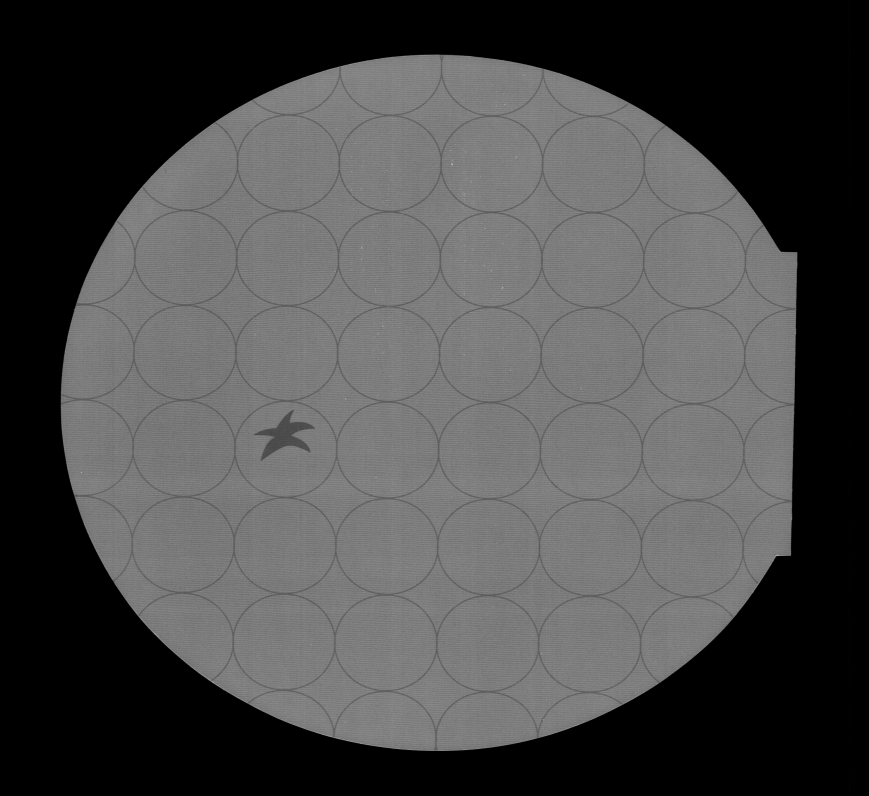